THE
ART
of the
FLASK

THE
ART
of the
FLASK

ENTERTAINING FROM THE HIP

PAUL KNORR

CIDER MILL PRESS

BOOK PUBLISHERS

KENNEBUNKPORT, MAINE

13-Digit ISBN: 9781604336986
10-Digit ISBN: 1604336986

This book may be ordered by mail from the publisher. Please include $5.99 for postage and handling.
Please support your local bookseller first!

Books published by Cider Mill Press Book Publishers are available at special discounts
for bulk purchases in the United States by corporations, institutions, and other organizations.
For more information, please contact the publisher.

Cider Mill Press Book Publishers
"Where good books are ready for press"
PO Box 454
12 Spring Street
Kennebunkport, Maine 04046

Visit us on the Web! www.cidermillpress.com

Cover and interior design by Alicia Freile, Tango Media
Typography: Bell MT, Castellar MT, Coneria Script, Handle Old Style, ITC Avant Garde

Photo Credits:
Page 12 & 186: W. C. Fields as Micawber from the 1935 film David Copperfield (Wikimedia Commons); page 24: Latest thing in flasks. Mlle. Rhea, dainty dancer who is now in the city as part of the Keiths program inaugurates the garter flask fad in Washington (Library of Congress Prints and Photographs Division, LC-DIG-ds-00150); pages 26-27: New York, New York. O'Reilly's bar on Third Avenue in the "Fifties" (Library of Congress Prints and Photographs Division, LC-DIG-fsa-8d21787); page 34: Oscar Wilde / Sarony. (Library of Congress Prints and Photographs Division, LC-DIG-ppmsca-49836); pages 48-49: Interior of a crowded bar moments before midnight, June 30, 1919, when wartime prohibition went into effect New York City (Library of Congress Prints and Photographs Division, LC-USZ62-123253); pages 158-159: Harry Kirivan drawing draft at bar inside his tavern (Library of Congress Prints and Photographs Division, LC-USZ62-115941); page 168: Hemingway posing for a dust jacket photo by Lloyd Arnold for the first edition of "For Whom the Bell Tolls", at the Sun Valley Lodge, Idaho, late 1939 (Wikimedia Commons); pages 170-171: Hooch Hound, a dog trained to detect liquor sniffs at flask in back pocket of man, seated, fishing on pier on the Potomac River (Library of Congress Prints and Photographs Division, LC-USZ62-96300); page 182: Portrait of Cab Calloway, Columbia studio, New York, N.Y., ca. Mar. 1947 (Wikimedia Commons); page 186: W. C. Fields as Micawber from the 1935 film David Copperfield. (Wikimedia Commons); pages 190-191: Scenes of open gambling in Reno, Nevada casinos: looking down crowded bar (Library of Congress Prints and Photographs Division, LC-USZ62-64633).

All other photographs used under official license from Shutterstock.com

Printed in China
1 2 3 4 5 6 7 8 9 0
First Edition

TABLE
OF
CONTENTS

INTRODUCTION

ART OF THE FLASK

The popularity of flasks has come and gone as fashion and laws have changed. Flasks have been with us for hundreds of years and once again, after their heyday during Prohibition, are making a comeback. In these uncertain economic times, the ability to purchase and carry your own supply of liquor still may make you seem like a lush—but you are a wise, discerning, and frugal lush.

Choosing the correct flask, as with any other fashion accessory, is no simple task. There are different styles of flasks for different purposes. If you're looking to casually produce a flask to spike your coffee like a hard-boiled private eye in a film noir, you're going to want an elegant, understated silver or stainless steel flask. If you are looking to sneak some booze into a stadium concert, you are less concerned with looks and more concerned with the metal detector and in need of a plastic flask or collapsible pouch. This book will guide you to the flask that fits your needs.

Once a flask has been selected, what should it be filled with? You can follow the tradition of our forefathers and stick with straight whiskey or you can go a different route with a classic cocktail. Included here are a large collection of classic cocktails, many of which can be traced back to Prohibition, the glory days of the flask. These older mixed drinks were stronger and less sweet with none of the syrupy flavorings found in so many drinks today, syrupy flavorings that will only gum up the inside of a flask. Of course, if you prefer to keep things simple, there is a collection of straight liquors that are worthy of filling your flask, including the traditional whiskey, brandy, and scotch as well as some that you might not have considered.

Now that you have your flask and have filled it with the libation of your choice, how do you make use of this glorious device without looking like a fool? Within these pages are a few simple guidelines regarding ways to make use of your flask without embarrassing yourself and without running too far afoul of the law. Then when the day is done, the flask will need to be cleaned out and made ready for the next adventure. Also included here are some tips and techniques to keep your flask clean and fresh.

Finally, included here is a brief history of the flask because no book dedicated to flasks could be complete without informing the reader of the essential part flasks have played in the human story. Flasks have been with us throughout history. They were sold at the gladiatorial games as clay souvenir flasks of wine with popular Roman gladiators embossed on the front. Cheap glass flasks filled with whiskey were given out at campaign stops with the faces of the candidates on them. During Prohibition, a vast number of flasks flooded the United States pushing the 18th Amendment into irrelevance, leading to the law's repeal. The part flasks have played in many of the societal and economic changes of the past several hundred years should be celebrated.

Whatever your reason for having a flask and for purchasing a book celebrating the flask, the aim of this book is to help you make the most of it and to enjoy it to the fullest. Drink well!

"Everybody's got to believe in something. I believe I'll have another drink."

—W.C. FIELDS

HISTORY
OF THE
FLASK

In a broad sense, a flask is anything that can be used to transport liquids. When looked at that way, flasks have been around since cavemen decided that bringing something to drink with them while hunting was a good idea. Early flasks were made of animal skins and bladders (sometimes literally the bladder, and sometimes the stomach). The skins would be cured and sealed using beeswax to keep them water tight and to give them more strength so they would last longer.

In pre-Christian times, many temples and holy sites had some special spring or pool visitors could bathe in or drink from to help with health, wealth, or other divine issues. Available for purchase were small ceramic flasks with an image of the patron god

or goddess so that visitors could bring some of those special waters back with them. The temple gained a source of income from the souvenir flasks. The worshipers would display their empty flasks to show their devotion. The Roman coliseums had an even more direct income stream from flasks. They would sell molded clay flasks filled with wine and showing images of famous gladiators during the games. Not too different from commemorative cup day at the ball park.

Before there could be what we think of as the pocket flask there needed to be two things: distilled alcohol and pockets. Around the 1600s, the clothing styles of the day provided men with internal pockets so that instead of carrying a purse tied to the belt, valuables could be kept hidden and more secure. As luck would have it, it was around this time that distilled alcohol was leaving the alchemist's laboratory and making its way to the common man. The improved distillation techniques made distilled alcohol safer and cheaper, and popular beverages such as whiskey, vodka, rum, and gin started to appear. Since

this new-fangled "hard liquor" was concentrated in its effects, not as much volume was needed as would be the case with wine or beer. One group of men who had a desire to carry their liquor with them and also had a ready-made container to keep it in was the professional soldier. Liquor could provide bravery before battle, could calm the nerves after battle, and could even be used as a disinfectant. In the days of muzzle-loading muskets, soldiers carried powder flasks, which were small metal or bone containers needed to carry gunpowder while keeping it dry and safe from sparks. Soldiers must have quickly realized that an extra powder flask filled with gin was a welcome ration while on the march.

Flasks as we think of them today started to take shape in the 19th century. In the early 1800s there was a sharp increase in glass production in the United States. Molten glass could be blown into metal molds to quickly produce flasks of different designs, colors, and sizes, all at very reasonable prices. These flasks had thick sides and oval shapes like flattened eggs, which let them fit easily into a pocket. Also popular were flasks that rounded and curved to lay better against the hip or leg, giving rise to the hip flasks as we would recognize

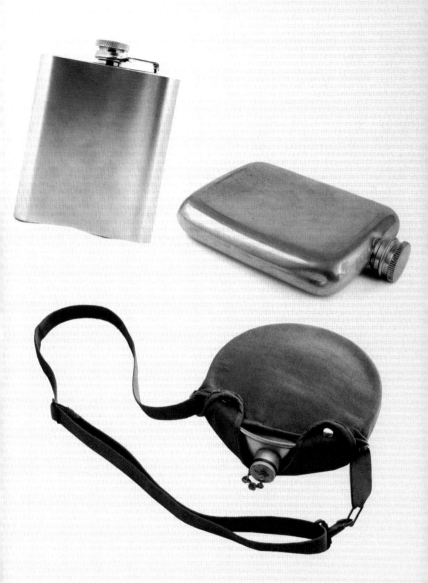

them today. Glass flasks could be purchased at taverns or general stores filled with whiskey and then refilled again from the shopkeeper's barrel. Flasks of this time would have images embossed on them. Popular designs were patriotic eagles, flags, and stars, as well as images of famous people. Flasks made of glass were so cheap that they could be given out (filled of course!) as advertising for anything from a liquor brand to a presidential candidate.

But now that flasks were so cheap and everyone had one, what was a poor aristocrat to do to show his status and wealth? The upper crust of society abandoned glass flasks in exchange for ones of metal, the more precious the better. Even then, gold was deemed a bit *too* ostentatious, but silver on the other hand was perfect. Silver also had the added benefit of improving the taste of the liquor. The rich also led the charge in inventing many of the improvements expected of today's flasks, including screw tops instead of corks to prevent leaks and hinged tops so the screw cap didn't get lost. In spite of the improvements, flasks were still considered an optional accessory. Sales of higher-end flasks stagnated until January 1920 when an event took place that made criminals out of many

Americans, giving them a very good reason to keep their liquor close and hidden.

Before Prohibition, the United States had a drinking problem. In the 1830s when glass flasks filled with whiskey were being handed out left and right, the average American over the age of 15 was drinking the equivalent of 90 bottles of 80 proof liquor per year or an average of four shots a day. Something needed to be done, and for better or worse the idea at the time was an outright ban on the sale, production, and transportation of alcohol. The fabric of American culture changed almost overnight. It was considered respectable for men and women to frequent speak-easies and other hidden clubs together for the first time. The presence of high government officials at many of these speak-easies helped to erode respect for the rule of law. It is also remembered as the golden age of the flask. The *Washington Herald* wrote in 1922: "Wholesale and retail dealers in silverware say that one bright spot in their business has been the demand for silver hip flasks. Hundreds of thousands have been bought for Christmas presents." Flasks became essential for anyone who wanted to consume alcohol outside the privacy of their own home. As Frank Kelly

Rich writes in "Pocket Full of Joy": "In the early days of Prohibition, before speakeasies began blossoming like desert roses, a flask wasn't just a thing to get you from one party to another, it *was* the party." Flasks also changed from the flashy display item a gentleman could casually produce to something that had to stay truly hidden—invisible to casual observers. Thus the start of the "novelty flask" or the flask that looks like anything but a flask. Anything that could be carried without arousing suspicion was eligible to be made into a hidden container for alcohol. Flasks were being used by so many people that by the late 1920s and early 1930s local police could no longer be bothered to arrest someone they suspected of carrying one. It was assumed that everyone had a flask so what was the point anymore?

By 1933 the whole country had had enough of Prohibition. It was not working, it caused more prob-lems than it solved, and it was repealed that December. After the repeal, there was no longer any reason to carry liquor around hidden in a flask. Flasks started to fade in popularity except for a few small groups. Soldiers of course kept their flasks just as they did 300 years before. On the silver screen, a private eye could be seen dragging out a flask and pouring a nip into his coffee, but the average American had left the flask behind. The cocktail or mixed drink had sprung up during Prohibition to mask the taste of poor quality liquor. Americans were exploring the cocktail craze with elaborate Polynesian concoctions and various other mixed drinks that made use of the dizzying array of liqueurs being introduced.

Today the wheel of time is turning back once again to those heady days of the 1830s. Americans may not be drinking the quantity that we did then, but the quality has improved substantially. Flasks have become less common and thus more interesting. A gentleman or lady at a party quietly taking a sip from a flask is no longer so common as to hardly be noticed. The defiance that a flask represented during Prohibition against what was thought to be a ridiculous law is back once again, railing against the price gouging of the local ball park. Soft plastic collapsible pouches and hard plastic flasks are being used to get around the metal detectors more and more commonly being used at concerts and sporting events. Like the flappers of the 1920s once sang: "Happy days are here again!"

The popularity of the flask rose during Prohibition in the United States when the concealment of spirits was necessary. In those days, women often carried a flask strapped by a garter to their thigh, where they were less likely to be frisked.

"THIS
MIGHT BE
WATER."

—ANONYMOUS

ENGRAVE THIS QUOTE ON
YOUR FAVORITE FLASK.

FLASK MATERIALS AND MAINTENANCE

Different Flask Materials

ANTIQUE OR VINTAGE

The golden age of the flask in the United States was from 1920 to 1933, also known as Prohibition. When liquor was made illegal, flasks came into fashion among all walks of life. Flasks from this time period were made from silver, pewter, steel, glass, and even copper. Silver flasks from the 1920s and 1930s have the

highest value for collectors, but hidden or disguised flasks can also command a high price because of their history. Flasks from the 1800s were frequently made of glass and are highly prized among collectors.

STAINLESS STEEL

Steel is by far the most common material used today to make flasks. Steel is strong, inexpensive, and resists corrosion. Stainless steel also won't retain flavors or odors, so with a quick rinse you can change the contents of your flask without a hint of what was in it yesterday.

LEATHER

In this case, leather refers to stainless steel covered in leather. The leather trim gives the flask a classier look but also adds bulk so the flask may not fit as well in a pocket. Leather can also be stamped and embossed with a monogram, a brand name, or the name of the bride and groom.

SILVER

Silver is considered to be the best material for flasks. Like stainless steel, it will not corrode and does not retain odors. Pure silver is thought by some to enhance the flavors of liquors such as whiskey, gin, and vodka. One drawback to silver is its tendency to tarnish so extra effort will be required to keep the flask looking like new.

PEWTER

Pewter, sometimes called "poor man's silver" is a mixture of tin, copper, and antimony or lead. Earlier versions of pewter contained lead but once the health effects of lead poisoning became known, antimony was added instead. Pewter flasks from before the 20th century are collectible but should be

for display only. Modern pewter flasks are perfectly safe and combine the shine and elegance of silver for a fraction of the cost.

GOLD PLATED

For something really flashy, there are gold plated flasks. Considering that a flask should be kept out of sight, the purpose of gold plating is questionable. It has been said that, like silver, gold enhances the flavor of the spirit, giving it a metallic taste.

PLASTIC

Flasks made from plastic or Nalgene are becoming more popular as more and more venues start using metal detectors to screen their guests. Plastic flasks allow liquor to be brought into concerts and onto cruise ships undetected. They are also cheap, do not retain odors, and do not affect the taste of the liquor.

GLASS

Glass is rarely used for flasks today but in the early 1800s with the boom in American glass production and the boom in American alcohol consumption, glass was a popular and inexpensive choice. Many antique collectible examples of early American glass liquor flasks can be found.

"WORK IS THE CURSE OF THE DRINKING CLASS."

—OSCAR WILDE

Different Types of Flasks

HIP FLASK

Hip flasks have curved bodies that conform to the shape of the holder's waist or thigh, making them easier to hide. They usually range in size from 5 to 9 ounces (150-270 ml).

POCKET FLASK

Pocket flasks have straight or flat bodies and are meant to be hidden in a pants pocket or in an outside suit pocket. They usually range in size from 5 to 9 ounces (150-270 ml).

TOP POCKET FLASK

Top pocket flasks are small and flat and are meant to be hidden in a shirt or inside jacket pocket. They usually range in size from 3 to 5 ounces (90-150 ml).

ROUND FLASK

As the name implies, these are round in shape. They are less noticeable under clothing and come in a variety of sizes.

PURSE FLASK

Purse flasks are larger and can be in a variety of shapes. Some can be as large as a quart (or liter). They are meant to be hidden in a women's purse but can be hidden in a backpack or suitcase as well.

COLLAPSIBLE

Collapsible flasks look like oversized Capri Sun–style juice pouches. They are lightweight and have soft plastic sides that can be flattened down after being emptied. They are available in a variety of sizes up to two liters.

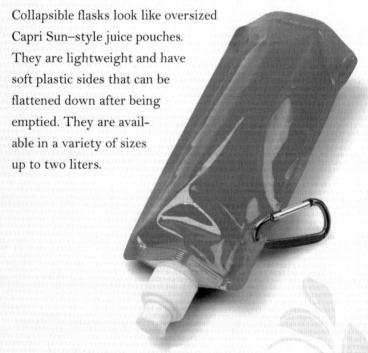

NOVELTY FLASK

Flasks that do not look like flasks. There are a wide variety of these, ranging from a flask shaped like a pair of binoculars to a flask shaped like an old Nintendo game cartridge. This type of flask was essential in the early days of Prohibition but they are really just for fun today. Flasks like these are more for display and not for carrying around.

"Always carry
a flagon of whiskey
in case of snake
bites. Furthermore,
always carry
a small snake."

—W.C. FIELDS

Funnels

If you use a flask, you need to fill it and for that you will need a funnel. Some flasks come with funnels built in as part of the base or as part of a carrying case. Other flasks will include a small metal funnel with the purchase of the flask but the funnel is not attached or stored with the flask. Of course a funnel can be quickly and easily crafted from a square of aluminum foil if a pre-made funnel is not available. The most ingenious funnels are the ones that not only are included with the flask but also are threaded so that they screw onto the top in place of the cap. These are great because the funnel won't tilt to the side or fall out while filling the flask. Of course, you will pay a premium for this kind of feature. The best funnel I have found for use with a flask is a simple cheap funnel I found at a dollar store. One small simple feature makes it great. Molded on the outside of the funnel are small rubber ridges that run from the top to the bottom. These not only grip the opening of the flask, they also provide a small gap between the funnel and flask for air to escape as the flask fills.

Flask Maintenance

Flasks are not meant to replace liquor bottles as a place to store booze. Liquor should not be kept in a flask for more than three days. After that, it starts to take on a metallic taste. Some suggest that the liquor left in the flask at the end of the day should be consumed as a nightcap before going to bed. That gives a clean start to the next day.

CLEANING METAL FLASKS

Never use soap to clean the inside of a flask. Soap, even dish soap, can leave a residue that gives a soapy flavor to anything put in it later. Here are the three simple, common products that work best to clean a flask:

1. Water

A rinse with plain water is the simplest and easiest way to clean out a flask. Fill the flask halfway with the hottest water you can stand. Close the cap and shake the flask for a few seconds before dumping out the water, then repeat at least twice more. Once the flask is well rinsed, allow it to air dry upside down with the cap open.

2. White Vinegar

If the flask has a funky odor or funny taste, a rinse with white vinegar might help to clean it out. Plain white vinegar can be found almost anywhere and is safe to drink although very acidic. Fill the flask halfway with vinegar, close the cap and shake for 30 seconds to a minute, then dump out the vinegar. Afterwards, rinse again multiple times with water, letting the flask dry upside down and with the cap open.

3. Lemon Juice

Lemon juice can also be used instead of vinegar. It is not as acidic but has a much more pleasant smell if any residue is left in the flask. Fresh lemon juice should be used instead of the bottled kind. The bottled juice frequently has added sugar which can lead to the growth of mold or mildew in the flask. Fill the flask a quarter to halfway with lemon juice, close the cap and shake for 30 seconds to a minute, then dump out the juice. Afterwards, rinse again multiple times with water, letting the flask dry upside down with the cap open.

CLEANING GLASS OR GLASS-LINED FLASKS

A great trick for cleaning the inside of a glass flask is to use a denture cleanser tablet. Put one tablet in the flask, breaking it into smaller pieces if it won't fit through the opening. Then, fill the flask about three quarters full with warm water and allow the denture cleaner to do its work. As the bubbles begin to die down, fill the flask the rest of the way to the top so all parts get cleaned. Do not close the cap while cleaning this way. The bubbles will cause pressure to build up inside the flask and it could burst.

"What whiskey will not cure, there is no cure for."

—PROVERB

FLASK ETIQUETTE

on't bring a flask somewhere that might get you fired. A party with friends is something altogether different from the Monday morning staff meeting. Whip out the flask at a party: "dashing rebel." Whip it out at the office: "Borderline alcoholic" and a call to HR.

Don't bring a flask to a place that sells alcohol at a reasonable price. Sneaking a flask of whiskey into the bar is akin to stealing and will likely get you thrown out. Note the "reasonable price" caveat. Sporting events and snooty expensive bars might be acceptable, but exercise caution and judgment.

Don't drive with a flask. If traveling in a car, place your flask in the trunk. A flask is considered an open container, and even if you have not yet had a sip, it can still get you in trouble. This applies to passengers as

well as the driver. Open container laws ban any open container of alcohol inside a vehicle.

Be prepared to share but don't overshare. Passing your flask is common courtesy within limits. Share only with close friends who are interested. You don't need to offer it to everyone. And if the offer is made and refused, do not under any circumstance try to apply pressure to partake.

Be discreet. Don't bring it out in public places or wave it around. Like a tie or sport coat, it is a fashion accessory that's at its best when it doesn't stand out. Discretion might keep you from being arrested as well as from looking like a fool. A flask is considered by law to be an open container of alcohol, so keep in mind that it is illegal to carry in most public places.

"TRUST ME, YOU CAN DANCE"

—VODKA

FLASK-WORTHY DRINKS

*M*any people are convinced that the flask is only for straight spirits: gin, vodka, bourbon, whiskey, Scotch, cognac, brandy, etc. This was the tradition for many years, and may still possibly be the right thing for you. But today, one can make almost anything—there are no rules! One can make cocktails in a shaker, for instance, and pour the resulting drink in their flask through a spout. How about making yourself a slightly dirty martini—just put in a few ice chips or leave it near an ice pack while you travel. Or how about a Rob Roy, Manhattan, or Cosmo? Your imagination is the only thing stopping you. Just make sure you clean your baby right after! You want to be able to make that same rebellious fashion statement is ready and usable the next time you suit up for fun with that same smirk of confidence!

Admiral Cocktail

2 parts Dry Gin
1 part Cherry Heering
1 part Fresh Lime Juice

Shake with ice and strain into
your flask using a funnel.

Alabama Slammer

1 part Southern Comfort
1 part Amaretto
1 part Cranberry Juice

Shake with ice and strain into
your flask using a funnel.

Alaska Cocktail

2 parts Gin
1 part Yellow Chartreuse
3 dashes Orange Bitters

Shake with ice and strain into
your flask using a funnel.

Americano

1 part Campari
1 part Sweet Vermouth
1 part Club Soda

Stir Campari and vermouth with
ice and strain into your flask using
a funnel. Top with club soda.

Astoria

1 part Gin
1 part Dry Vermouth
4 dashes Campari

Shake with ice and strain into
your flask using a funnel.

Astropop

1 part Cherry Vodka
1 part Coconut Vodka
1 part Peppermint
Schnapps
1 part Cranberry Juice

Shake with ice and strain into
your flask using a funnel.

B & B

1 part Benedictine
1 part Brandy

Using a funnel, fill your flask halfway
with Benedictine and then top it off
with your favorite brandy.

Bat Juice

4 parts Cranberry Juice
1 part Bacardi Black Rum

Shake with ice and strain into
your flask using a funnel.

Black Dog

3 parts Bourbon
1 part Sweet Vermouth
1 part Blackberry Brandy

Shake with ice and strain into
your flask using a funnel.

Blue Kamikaze

1 part Blue Curaçao
1 part Vodka
1 part Fresh Lime Juice

Shake with ice and strain into
your flask using a funnel.

Bourbon Bender

1 part Bourbon
1 part Amaretto
1 part Fresh Lime Juice

Shake with ice and strain into
your flask using a funnel.

Cactus Jack

1 part Whiskey
1 part Pineapple Vodka
1 part Orange Juice

Shake with ice and strain into
your flask using a funnel.

Casino

4 parts Gin
1 part Maraschino Liqueur
1 part Lemon Juice
4 dashes Orange Bitters

Shake with ice and strain into
your flask using a funnel.

Classic Gin and Tonic

1 part Tanqueray Gin
1 part Tonic Water
Splash of Lime Juice

Pour Tanqueray and tonic water into flask using a funnel. Top with a splash of lime juice.

Cloister

1 part Gin
1 part Grapefruit Juice

Using a funnel, fill your flask
halfway with gin and then
top it off with grapefruit juice
or pink grapefruit juice.

Corpse Reviver #2

Dash Absinthe
1 part Gin
1 part Cointreau
1 part Lillet Blanc
1 part Lemon Juice

Pour the dash of absinthe into
the flask, swish it around to coat the
inside and pour it out. Shake the
remaining ingredients with ice
and strain into your flask
using a funnel.

Cosmopolitan

2 parts Vodka
1 part Cointreau
1 part Cranberry Juice
1 part Lime Juice

Shake with ice and strain into
your flask using a funnel.

Fire Cracker

1 part Tequila
1 part Fireball Cinnamon
Whiskey
Tabasco Sauce to taste

Shake the tequila and Fireball
with ice and strain into your
flask using a funnel. Top with
Tabasco to taste.

Flask-
O-Happiness

1 part Raspberry, Blackberry
or Strawberry Vodka
1 part Pineapple Juice
1 part Lime Juice
Splash 7-Up

Shake equal parts vodka,
pineapple juice, and lime juice
with ice and strain into your flask
using a funnel. Top off with
a splash of 7-Up.

Four Fellows

1 part White Rum
1 part Dark Rum
1 part Spiced Rum
1 part Coconut Rum

Add all ingredients to flask using
funnel. Enjoy slowly.

Frisco

2 parts Rye
1 part Lemon Juice
Splash Benedictine

Shake with ice and strain into
your flask using a funnel.

Godfather

2 parts Scotch
1 part Amaretto

Shake with ice and strain into
your flask using a funnel.

Godmother

2 parts Vodka
1 part Amaretto

Shake with ice and strain into your
flask using a funnel.

Golddigger

1 part Whiskey
1 part Goldschläger

Shake with ice and strain into
your flask using a funnel.

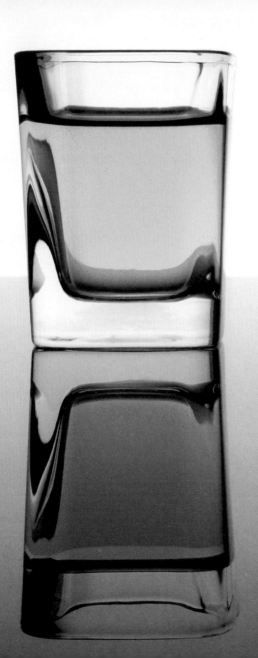

Gold Furnace

1 part Fireball Cinnamon
Whiskey
1 part Goldschläger
Tabasco Sauce

Shake the Fireball and
Goldschläger with ice and strain
into your flask using a funnel.
Top with Tabasco to taste.

Grape Chill

2 parts Grape Vodka
1 part Vanilla Vodka
1 part Pineapple Juice

Shake with ice and strain into
your flask using a funnel.

Grape Sourball

1 part Grape Vodka
1 part Crystal Light
Lemonade
1 part Orange Juice

Shake with ice and strain into
your flask using a funnel.

Head Rush

1 part Peach Vodka
1 part Pear Vodka
1 part Sambuca

Shake with ice and strain into
your flask using a funnel.

Liquid Crack

1 part Jägermeister
1 part Peppermint Schnapps
1 part 151 Proof Rum
1 part Fireball Cinnamon
Whiskey

Shake with ice and strain into
your flask using a funnel.

Manhattan

2 parts Rye Whiskey
1 part Sweet Vermouth

Shake with ice and strain into
your flask using a funnel.

Martini

3 parts Dry Gin
1 part Dry Vermouth

Shake with ice and strain into
your flask using a funnel.

Massive Mounds

1 part Chocolate Vodka
1 part Coconut Vodka

Shake with ice and strain into
your flask using a funnel.

Nasty Stewardess

1 part Orange Vodka
1 part Licor 43
1 part Tonic Water

Shake equal parts of orange vodka
and Licor 43 (also known as
Cuarenta y Tres) with ice and
strain into your flask using a funnel,
leaving the flask two-thirds full.
Top off with chilled tonic water.

Negroni

2 parts Gin
1 part Campari
1 part Dry Vermouth
2 dashes Orange Bitters

Shake with ice and strain into your flask
using a funnel.

Prairie Wildfire

1 part Tequila
Tabasco Sauce to taste

Add tequila to flask using funnel.
Top with Tabasco Sauce
to taste.

Preakness

4 parts Rye
1 part Benedictine
1 part Sweet Vermouth
4 dashes Angostura Bitters

Shake with ice and strain into
your flask using a funnel.

Red Head

1 part Jägermeister
1 part Peach Schnapps
1 part Cranberry Juice

Shake with ice and strain into
your flask using a funnel.

Rob Roy

2 parts Scotch
1 part Sweet Vermouth

Shake with ice and strain into
your flask using a funnel.

Rusty Nail

3 parts Scotch
1 part Drambuie

Shake with ice and strain into
your flask using a funnel.

Siberian Mouthwash

1 part Vodka
1 part 100 proof Peppermint Schnapps

Using a funnel, fill your flask halfway with vodka and then top it off with peppermint schnapps. The sugar in lower-proof schnapps might make the cap of your flask sticky.

Sidecar

2 parts Brandy
1 part Lemon Juice
1 part Triple Sec

Shake with ice and strain into
your flask using a funnel.

Snake Bite

4 parts Canadian Whisky
1 part Fresh Lime Juice

Shake with ice and strain into
your flask using a funnel.

Southern Blues

3 parts Southern Comfort
1 part Black Haus
Blackberry Schnapps

Shake with ice and strain into
your flask using a funnel.

Spitfire

1 part Whiskey
1 part Dark Rum
1 part Cherry Vodka

Shake with ice and strain into
your flask using a funnel.

Stinger

3 parts Brandy
1 part White Crème de
Menthe

Shake with ice and strain into
your flask using a funnel.

Temptation

2 parts Rye Whiskey
1 part Dubonnet Blonde
1 part Triple Sec
1 part Pernod

Shake with ice and strain into
your flask using a funnel.

Third Rail

1 part Light Rum
1 part Cherry Brandy
1 part Calvados
Dash Pernod

Shake with ice and strain into
your flask using a funnel.

Tropical Storm

1 part White Rum
1 part Dark Rum
1 part Passion Fruit Syrup
Splash of Lemon Juice

Shake with ice and strain into
your flask using a funnel.

Twisted Gimlet

2 parts Gin
1 part Triple Sec
2 drops Orange Bitters

Stir with ice and strain into
your flask using a funnel.

Waldorf

2 parts Bourbon
1 part Pernod
1 part Sweet Vermouth
3 dashes Angostura Bitters

Shake with ice and strain into
your flask using a funnel.

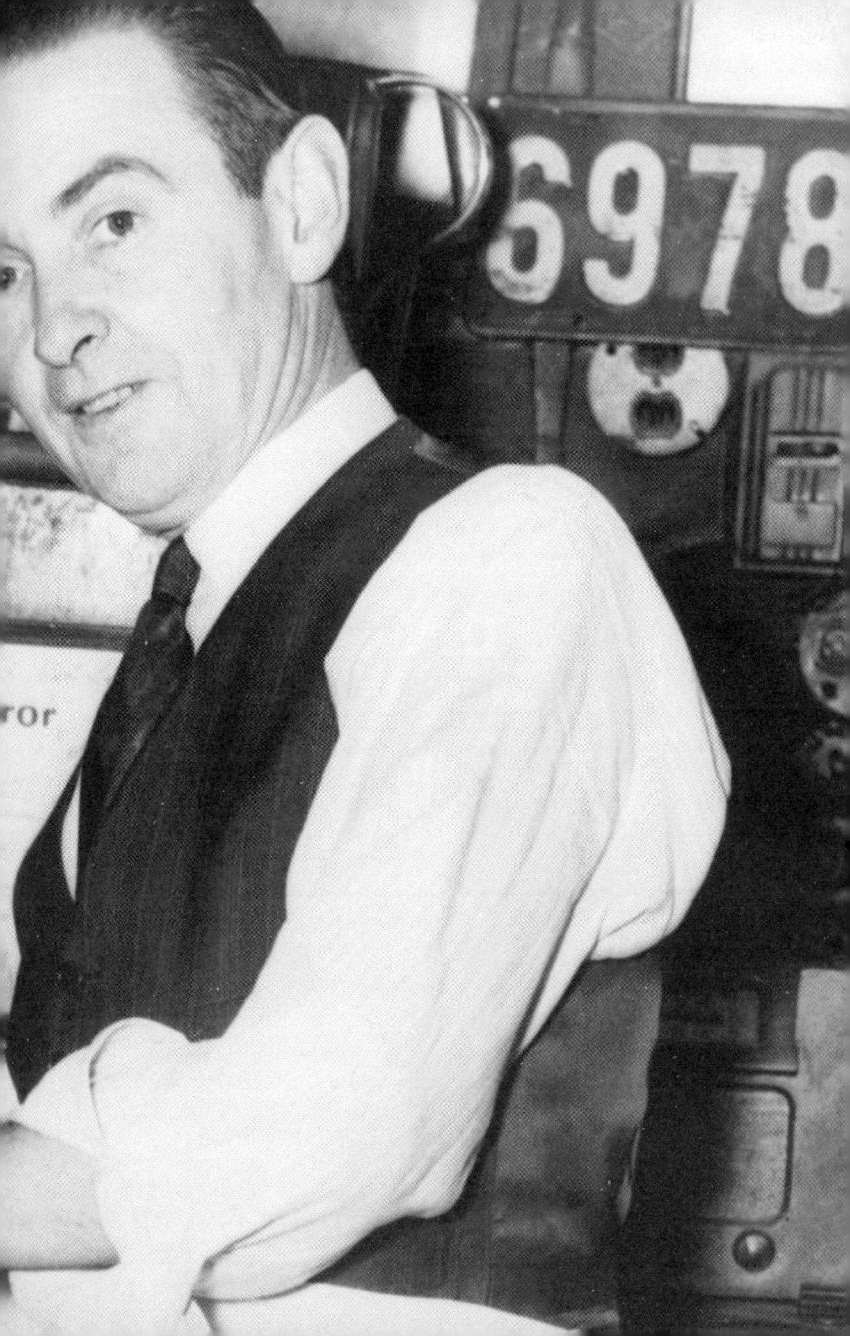

6978

MIXERS

When you're on the go, never sacrifice a quality cocktail! These mixers are perfect accompaniments to your preferred liquor, and are usually quite accessible. Pair the contents of your handy flask and with any of these simple options, and your day will be made.

COFFEE

This is the classic flask maneuver: Fish your flask out of its hiding place and pour an ounce or two of Irish whiskey into your coffee. Breakfast (or your day in your office) just got a little brighter. Coffee is a great mixer for whiskey, vodka, or rum.

TEA

Perhaps you're not a coffee drinker. In that case, pour a dollop of liquor from your flask into your tea. Whiskey, rum, and gin are great in hot tea. Vodka, tequila, and rum work great with iced tea.

COLA

The dark color of cola provides perfect cover for almost any liquor you want to keep in your flask. Of course, cola also tastes great with almost any alcohol. I don't recommend tequila (not my favorite) but rum and whiskey both blend perfectly with cola.

ORANGE JUICE

So you've already added a shot to your coffee. Why not make a screwdriver part of your balanced breakfast? Whiskey, rum, and especially vodka all work well with orange juice.

BEER

This is for those for whom beer just doesn't do the job fast enough. Turn your beer into a boilermaker by adding a shot of whiskey from your flask. Keep in mind that flask etiquette dictates that you should never pour from your flask in an establishment that sells alcohol at reasonable prices.

FRUIT PUNCH

Want to sneak a drink at a child's birthday party? Pollute your cup of innocent fruit punch with a shot form you well-hidden flask. Clear liquors such as rum and vodka work well flavorwise and keep themselves hidden in the punch. A word of caution: Drunkenness at children's birthday parties is frowned upon (trust me) so don't let it get out of hand.

LEMONADE

A tall glass of lemonade is refreshing on a hot summer day but add a shot or two from your flask to make it even better. Clear liquors work best, including vodka and flavored vodkas, rum, and gin.

CRANBERRY JUICE

Is there any breakfast beverage that cannot be improved with a shot from a flask? (Yes: milk.) But, like orange juice and fruit punch, cranberry juice is a perfect mixer for clear liquors like vodka, rum, gin, and tequila.

ORANGE SODA

Here is where you need to branch out into the flavored vodkas. Orange soda with a shot of vanilla vodka makes a terrific creamsicle. Orange soda with fruit flavors like mango, papaya, and guava turn a vending machine staple into a tropical cocktail. If you're trying to keep it on the down low, don't put in any paper umbrellas.

GINGER ALE

Here is another versatile mixer that will work with any liquor. Whiskey, rum, gin, vodka, and tequila all work great with ginger ale.

"Always do sober what you said you'd do drunk. That will teach you to keep your mouth shut."

—ERNEST HEMINGWAY

SPIRITS FOR YOUR FLASK

THE SANTA TERESA 1796 RUM

A rum produced in Venezuela using a copper pot still and aged in bourbon barrels initially before being further aged in a solera system (like a fine sherry). The rum has a spiciness to it like a rye whiskey but rounds it out with notes of honey and smoke. Drinking it warm helps to heighten the sweetness, making it perfect for a flask.

BLENDED SCOTCH

The smoky flavor of scotch comes from the Scottish process of drying the malted barley over a peat fire. Blended scotch means that several different distillates from different years are blended together to create a

consistent and flavorful scotch. Blended scotch makes
for a perfect flask filler because the vanilla, peat, and
smoke flavors will pair well with coffee or ginger ale
but can be enjoyed straight as well. Single malt scotch
can be transported in a flask especially when the bottle
is almost empty, but it has been said that the shaking
from walking and the body heat "bruise" the liquor.

JACK DANIEL'S WHISKEY

This is a well-rounded American whiskey with hints of butterscotch and spice, with a strong taste of pepper and smoke. Jack Daniels has the mash bill of bourbon with 84% corn but adds a secondary step after distilling in which the bourbon is filtered through stacks of sugar maple charcoal. The sugar maple charcoal helps to mellow the whiskey, making is smooth and easy to drink.

JAMESON IRISH WHISKEY

Irish whiskey does not use peat smoke to dry the malt and therefore lacks the smokiness characteristic of scotch, giving the whiskey a sweeter, gentler profile. An essential ingredient in Irish coffee, Jameson is also great with ginger ale and as a straight sipping whiskey.

TEQUILA

Good sipping tequilas such as those from Patron, Milagro, or Herradura, are often unfairly overlooked as flask-worthy spirits. Añejo (or "aged") tequila has been aged in charred oak barrels just like a whiskey or bourbon. The aging process softens the harshness commonly associated with tequila, leaving a strong agave flavor balanced out with oak, herbal, and citrus notes, along with a slightly bitter edge. These tequilas are meant to be sipped and savored and are perfect for a flask.

COGNAC

Cognac is made in a process very similar to whiskey, and, like whiskey, is an excellent spirit to keep in a flask. Cognacs are distilled from white wine, distilled twice in copper pot stills, and then aged in French oak casks. Popular examples of cognac include Hennessy, Remy Martin, and Courvoisier, but there are many other lesser-known brands that deserve a try.

VODKA

Vodka is tasteless, colorless, and odorless… making it perfect for a flask since it makes the task of cleaning the flask so much easier. In Eastern Europe and Russia, a flask of vodka would be perfectly appropriate, but it may seem unusual to the American palate. Vodka can seem a bit harsh to drink warm and straight from the flask, so mixing it with a breakfast orange juice or with hot tea might be a better option.

CALVADOS

Calvados is a French apple brandy made by distilling fermented apple cider. It has the strength of a brandy, often bottled at 90 proof or more, and the subtle aromas, flavors, and sweetness of apples. Calvados, or its American cousin Applejack, would be great in a flask on a cold winter night. A small pinch of cinnamon can be added to a flask of Applejack for the taste of apple pie.

FIREBALL

Fireball, a product of the Sazerac Companay, starts as a Canadian whisky. Cinnamon flavoring and sugar are added to produce a spirit that tastes much like the candy of the same name. Fireball's popularity has exploded in the United States and the spirit can be found in any liquor store. It is bottled at 66 proof so it is much lower in alcohol than most other spirits on this list.

It is perfect for a flask because it tastes great straight and can be mixed with many other things. Be careful with Fireball and some metal flasks because it might be hard to get the cinnamon smell out of the flask. The added sugar makes it important that the flask be cleaned nightly.

PEPPERMINT SCHNAPPS

In this case, I am referring to the traditional German style of schnapps which is very dry and very high in alcohol, not the sticky sweet version sold in most American liquor stores. Peppermint Schnapps is bottled at between 80 and 120 proof and has no sugar added to it. It has a bracingly strong peppermint flavor and an intense alcohol burn and leaves your breath clean and frosty. As with Fireball, the peppermint scent might stick around a bit if the schnapps is left in the flask overnight. Also be sure to stay away from any schnapps less than 80 proof; they will be syrupy and sweet and will gum up the inside of a flask.

"That last drink was a mess."

—CAB CALLOWAY

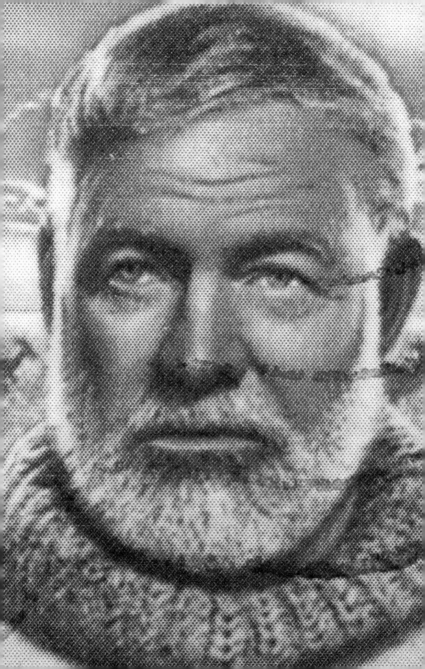

FAMOUS
FLASKS

JINNY, THE FLASK BELONGING TO ERNEST HEMINGWAY

Ernest Hemingway had a tall silver flask that he referred to by the name of Jinny. Many have speculated that Jinny referred to Jinny Pfeiffer, the younger sister of Hemingway's second wife, Pauline. It was rumored that Hemingway was having an affair with Jinny, but there were also rumors that Jinny preferred the company of women. Hemingway writes of Jinny (his flask) in his semi-fictional biography *True at First Light*: "The Jinny flask was in one pocket of the old Spanish double cartridge pouches. It was a pint bottle of Gordon's we had bought at Sultan Hamud and it was named after another old famous silver flask that had finally opened its seams at too many thousand feet during a war and had caused me to believe for a moment that I had been hit in the buttocks."

W. C. FIELDS

W.C. Fields made his career playing a hard-drinking scoundrel and apparently imitated the character he played in real life as well. Fields started his career as a Vaudeville juggler and did not drink at all since it would interfere with his act. But his role in the movie *International House* gave him a reputation as a heavy drinker, and Fields played up the role in his personal life. Phil Silvers, who had minor roles in some of Fields' movies, tells a story of an incident during the filming of *Tales of Manhattan* in 1942 where the producers pleaded with Fields not to drink while they were shooting because they were behind schedule. Fields responded: "Gentlemen, this is only lemonade. For a little acid condition afflicting me." He then handed the flask to Silvers to taste. Silvers

tasted that it was pure gin but told the producers that it was lemonade.

FRANK SINATRA

Frank Sinatra is rumored to be buried with a flask of his favorite drink, Jack Daniel's, in his pocket. He was also supposedly buried with a pack of Camels, his Zippo lighter, and 10 dimes. He had carried 10 dimes in his pocket since the kidnapping of his son in 1963, saying that he always wanted them handy in case he needed to make a phone call. His daughter Tina placed the dimes in his pocket. The whiskey was placed by Tina's sister Nancy.

MASONIC FLASK

In March 2016, the Norman C. Heckler auction house sold a rare Masonic flask for $56,160, thought to be one of the highest prices paid for a historic flask. The flask featured the square and star Masonic symbol as well as a "crossed keys" Masonic symbol. It was made between 1820 and 1830 by Covington Glassworks in Connecticut. At the same auction, a rare flask bearing a portrait of George Washington sold for $49,140.

GEORGE WASHINGTON

Like most people in his time, George Washington was a regular drinker. Beer, rum, and wine were all much safer to drink than water. He was known to drink a bottle of Madeira with dinner as well as the occasional nip of rum or glass of punch. The bar tab for his farewell party from the Constitutional Convention, dated September 15, 1787, gives a good idea of the drink that could be packed away by men of his stature: for 55 guests there was provided 54 bottles of Madeira, 60 bottles of Claret, 22 bottles of Port, and seven large bowls of punch. The total for the event came to 89 pounds, 4 shillings, and 2 pence, or what would be about $13,000 today.

In paintings of Washington, there is often a serving flask nearby or on a table behind General Washington. Because of the rising Temperance movement that would lead to Prohibition, later reproductions of these paintings sometimes omitted the flask, literally whitewashing the drinking that was common at the time.

THE LAST NIGHT
OF OPEN GA[...]
© 1910 BILLEVIT[...]

GLOSSARY
OF
INGREDIENTS

Absinthe

A high-proof (45-75% alcohol by volume) anise-flavored spirit made from several herbs and flowers including the flowers and leaves of the *Artemisia absinthium*, also called wormwood. Sale of Absinthe was banned in most of the world between 1907 and 1915. By the 1990s, research had shown that it was not as harmful as originally thought. Production was allowed again with over 200 brands available today.

Amaretto

An Italian liqueur made from apricot kernels and seeds and almond extract steeped in brandy and sweetened with sugar syrup. Amaretto is Italian for "a little bitter."

Angostura Bitters

Originally marketed as patented medicine, Angostura Bitters is a bitter-tasting herbal flavoring now used principally in food and cocktail recipes. Angostura was named for the town of Angostura in Venezuela. It contains no angostura bark, a medicinal bark which is named after the same town. Angostura Bitters is the most widely distributed bar item in the world.

Benedictine

A brandy-based herbal liqueur produced in France. Benedictine is believed to be the oldest liqueur continuously made, having first been developed by Dom Bernardo Vincelli in 1510 at the Benedictine Abbey of Fécamp in Normandy. Every bottle of Benedictine carries the initials "D.O.M." which stand for "Deo Optimo Maximo," or in English, "To God, most good, most great."

Bourbon

An American form of whiskey made from at least 51% corn, with the remainder being wheat or rye and malted barley. It is distilled to no more than 160 proof and aged in new charred white oak barrels for at least two years. It must be put into the barrels at no more than 125 U.S. proof; in this way it is similar to Scotch Whisky, which is also aged in charred barrels.

Brandy

A strong alcoholic spirit distilled from wine or fermented fruit juice.

Calvados

An apple brandy from the French region of Lower Normandy.

Campari

A branded alcoholic beverage (between 20-24% alcohol by volume) introduced in Italy in 1860 by Gaspare Campari. It is a mild bitters-type aperitif, often drunk with soda, orange juice, or in mixed drinks.

Canadian Whisky

A beverage distilled from fermented grain and aged in oak casks. The location, grain, type of oak, and length of the aging time all affect the flavor of the whisky.

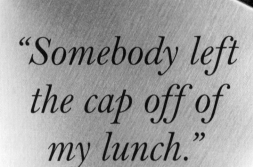

"*Somebody left the cap off of my lunch.*"

—W.C. FIELDS

Cherry Heering

A proprietary Danish cherry liqueur with a brandy base that has been produced since 1818 under several different names, including "Heering," "Peter Heering," and "Cherry Heering."

Cointreau

A fine, colorless, orange-flavored liqueur made from the dried skins of Curaçao oranges grown on the island of the same name in the Dutch West Indies. The generic term is Curaçao, and if redistilled and clarified is called triple sec.

Drambuie

A famous whiskey liqueur consisting of Highland malt scotch whiskey, heather honey, and herbs.

Dry Vermouth

A fortified wine flavored with aromatic herbs and spices. Dry vermouth is clear or pale yellow in color and very dry in flavor.

Dubonnet Blonde

A brand of quinquennial, a sweetened fortified aperitif wine that contains quinine. Produced in France, it comes in two varieties, Blonde and Rouge. Blonde is lighter in color and is less sweet than the Rouge.

Gin

Gin begins as a neutral spirit. It is then redistilled with or filtered through juniper berries and botanicals such as coriander seed, cassia bark, orange peels, fennel seeds, anise, caraway, angelica root, licorice, lemon peel, almonds, cinnamon bark, bergamot, and cocoa. It is this secondary process that imparts to each gin its particular taste.

Light Rum

A liquor made from fermented and distilled sugar cane juice or molasses. Clear in color and dry in flavor.

Lillet Blanc

An aperitif wine from the Bordeaux region of France. Lillet Blanc is the white variety that is pale yellow in color.

Maraschino Liqueur

A semi-dry Italian white cherry liqueur made from the Marasca cherry of Dalmatia, Croatia. This liqueur is sometimes used in sours in place of sugar. It tastes and looks nothing like the bright red Maraschino cherries.

Orange Bitters

A bitter-tasting herbal flavoring made from the rinds of unripe oranges. Originally marketed as a patent medicine and now principally used as a flavoring in food recipes and cocktails.

Peppermint Schnapps

Distilled from fermented grain with peppermint leaves added to steep before distillation or as part of a second distillation. Real schnapps has no sugar or flavoring added as the flavor should originate from the base material. Many syrupy sweet fruit liqueurs are labeled as schnapps but are not true schnapps because they add both sugar and flavorings.

Pernod

A semi-sweet anise flavored liqueur produced to be a substitute for absinthe without the wormwood. Produced by the Pernod-Ricard company.

Rye Whiskey

A beverage distilled from fermented grain that must be at least 51% rye and aged in oak casks.

Scotch

A beverage distilled from fermented grain and aged in oak casks. It must be produced in Scotland. Most varieties of scotch use peat smoke to dry the damp malt before fermentation, giving scotch its distinctive smoky flavor.

Sweet Vermouth

A fortified wine flavored with aromatic herbs and spices. Sweet vermouth is red in color and sweet in flavor.

Triple Sec

A highly popular flavoring agent in many drinks, triple sec is the best known form of curaçao, a liqueur made from the skins of the curaçao orange.

Vodka

A neutral spirit that can be distilled from almost anything that will ferment (grain, potato, grapes, corn, and beets). It is distilled multiple times and filtered to

"This End Up."

—ANONYMOUS

ENGRAVE THIS ON THE BOTTOM
OF YOUR FAVORITE FLASK.

remove as many of the impurities as possible. It is then diluted with water to bring the alcohol content down before being bottled. Vodka is also found in a wide variety of flavors, from bison grass to watermelon.

White Crème de Menthe

A very sweet, clear mint-flavored liqueur.

Yellow Chartreuse

A famous herbal French liqueur still produced by the Carthusian monks in France from a formula dating back to 1605 and containing 130 herbs and spices. Chartreuse comes in two varieties, Green and Yellow. Yellow is lower in alcohol than Green and it has a milder and sweeter flavor.

"*I feel sorry for people who don't drink. When they wake up in the morning, that's as good as they're going to feel all day.*"

—FRANK SINATRA

INDEX

ABOUT CIDER MILL PRESS
BOOK PUBLISHERS

Good ideas ripen with time. From seed to harvest,
Cider Mill Press brings fine reading, information,
and entertainment together between the covers of its
creatively crafted books. Our Cider Mill bears fruit twice
a year, publishing a new crop of titles each spring and fall.

"Where Good Books Are Ready for Press"

Visit us on the Web at
www.cidermillpress.com
or write to us at
PO Box 454
Kennebunkport, Maine 04046